H A M L Y N
C R E A T I V E   C R A F T S

MAKING
JEWELLERY

HAMLYN
CREATIVE CRAFTS

♦

MAKING JEWELLERY

Juliane Niemeier and Jürgen Klein

HAMLYN

Contents

A set (bracelet and necklace) made from rubber. Small metal tubes have been slipped over the individual strands, forming a complete ring in the case of the bracelet.

Introduction

Exclusive costume jewellery is a topic we have been fascinated by for a long while and we are convinced that you too will quickly come to enjoy making your own jewellery. After many years working in our bead shop we are only too familiar with the problems which may occur when making jewellery. In this book we have compiled useful tips for creating jewellery and important techniques.

As you will see, if you just apply a little imagination most things are very simple to make, and we have deliberately avoided very complicated techniques.

In particular we have made sure that all the pieces of jewellery require few tools and can be made in a relatively short time. The idea is that you should be able to wear and enjoy something unique and fashionable each day and on every special occasion.

It may well be that within a short while one or other of the materials is no longer available anywhere, because even individual beads are frequently subject to the demands of fashion. This is why in some cases we have deliberately shown how the character of a piece of jewellery can be both retained and totally altered by some small adaptation.

Try your hand first of all with some of the easier instructions. After initial small successes it won't be long before you decide you could 'just quickly' make a new necklace or new earrings, especially if you have a well-stocked shop nearby.

You will probably then go for more exotic creations and should you wonder how to go about doing something properly, that's the time to check up techniques in this book.

We hope you enjoy designing and making your own exclusive jewellery.

Julianne Niemeier and Jürgen Klein

Brief history of jewellery

Long before our ancestors began wearing clothes they painted their bodies and decorated themselves with a wide variety of things. Initially they used grasses, parts of plants and feathers but soon these were augmented by the teeth and bones of animals, plus fruit stones and shells. The urge for adornment led to the use of ever new materials and extensive refining of techniques. The discovery of metals meant the addition of vital raw materials which could be used in pieces of jewellery. Moreover, metal tools enabled jewellery to be made more easily and successfully.

Gold was a much-sought-after precious metal but it was not used for the manufacture of jewellery in all societies. Yellow alloys such as brass and bronze were frequently the basic materials in necklaces, rings or bracelets. One must also not forget to mention silver. High quality wrought silver work originates for example in ancient Islamic culture.

In many societies jewellery was not used merely for adornment, it also conveyed messages about the wearer, symbolising for example power, rank and the tribe to which he or she belonged.

The history of a tribe can frequently be traced through the traditional manufacture of jewellery and the use of certain symbols and patterns. One must however beware of assuming that, on the basis of the raw material or the technique used, this or that ethnic group always manufactured its jewellery in the same way. Red Indian bead embroidery only reached its peak after explorers and conquerors brought along glass beads as presents for their hosts and as a means of bartering. Jewellery increasingly acquired the status of a currency. This was very practical because it was very small and light. It could, for example, easily be carried great distances for bartering. Columbus took the cowrie shell to America because even in those days this translucent shell was an accepted means of payment.

Glass beads were of great economic value from ancient times because they were used for trading. For over 2,500 years necklaces of glass beads were accepted as a means of payment throughout the whole of Africa. One of the oldest glass beads is the Aggry pearl, considered valuable as early as Ancient Egyptian times. The most famous 'money bead' is the millefiori bead which was probably first manufactured by the Phoenicians.

The basic process used in the manufacture of these beads was constantly being refined by individual masters, reaching the most fantastic variations so that the individual beads became treasures in themselves.

Even a hundred years ago unusual chevron designs still had a high purchasing power. In earlier times these items were associated

Millefiori ('thousand flowers') beads.

with the sad story of slavery. A man's life was often worth only one bead. From this perspective it can be understood that whole countries were purchased with glass beads.

Trading with items made of glass was of the greatest economic and also political relevance. The supremacy and prosperity of Venice over hundreds of years, for example, was founded not only on sea trade but also on the secrets of glass-blowing.

The craft of glass-making in Bohemia, on which our costume jewellery industry of today is based, is relatively young.

In the area of the Iser mountains farmers of German origin who had been forcibly resettled on the barren land were unable to find any solid basis for their existence, but the rich woodland lent itself to commercial exploitation. In the 16th century the first glassworks came into being. Owing to the difficult location and poor roads the glass had to be processed on the spot to make end products which could be easily transported. This provided the impulse for an industry in small glass articles, which experienced such a boom that soon the name of the district capital Gablonz was associated world-wide with high quality glassware.

Initially only beads and other haberdashery items were manufactured. The special production of 'imitation jewellery' began in the 18th century and was an incredible success. Thanks to the influx of workers the population in Gablonz multiplied tenfold within a hundred years. In 1912 Lloyd's Register of Shipping in Trieste commissioned a steamer solely for the purpose of shipping costume jewellery from Gablonz to destinations overseas. The first slump came with World War 1, which blocked all the trading routes.

Just as the industry had managed to recover, World War 2 brought about its final collapse: factories and private property were expropriated and many plants were dismantled. The German-origin minority were intimidated by arrests and forced deportations. But many of the old traditional secrets of glass-making were saved. Capitalising on this knowledge a large number of jewellery manufacturers found a new home near Kaufbeuren. A new industry for costume jewellery was painstakingly established in Neugablonz, and one which once again enjoys an international reputation. Items made in Kaufbeuren-Neugablonz can be found in all the well-known fashion markets such as Paris, Milan and New York. Exports to almost 150 countries world-wide have been recorded.

The old contacts with Czechoslovakia have never been entirely broken off though. The industry which has been re-established there remains one of Europe's major suppliers of glass beads.

Some years ago Japan, with its low-priced, good quality jewellery, and Hong Kong, with its cheap jewellery, were feared competitors in the European costume jewellery industry. Today Taiwan is also an important supplier of cheap goods. Jewellery made according to traditional African designs is finding increasing acceptance on the European costume jewellery market.

But European manufacturers, with their feeling for trends and good design, are nevertheless sure of a firm place in this important sector of the economy.

A collage of older necklaces of Indian and African origin which are no longer made. Materials: glass, brass, silver and amber (above).

This white and coloured collar embroidered with glass beads is around 30 years old. It originates from the Ndebele tribe in South Africa.

This decorative fan embroidered with glass beads comes from India and is between 50 and 80 years old.

A thousand and one different beads

1

2

3

As soon as you start looking at the subject more closely you will be amazed at the endless variety of shapes and materials suitable for costume jewellery. At this point we would like to give you a brief overview of the most common materials used.

Initially the only materials available for the manufacture of jewellery were natural ones, which could be fashioned using simple tools. Many of these materials are used even today for costume jewellery and they are still as fascinating as ever. For this reason we have devoted an entire chapter to them.

Soon mankind was able to shape and harden clay. Excavation finds prove the early use of ceramics in pieces of jewellery. Today ceramic beads, usually fashioned by hand, still retain their attraction. The very fact that they are individually manufactured, often with an uneven surface, produces an irregularity of shape that adds charm. Creative possibilities using glazing and painting are very extensive. Unfortunately ceramic beads are very heavy and also sensitive to impact.

A further very important material is glass. We have already described the history and economic significance of this material on pages 6/7. No doubt you are familiar with the small rocailles, also referred to as Indian beads, and also with glass bugles and the cut glass drops used in crystal chandeliers. Here, though, we are dealing with very different types of glass beads.

The composition of the individual types of glass is a well-guarded manufacturer's secret. Certain amounts of mineral elements are added to the glass in order to achieve the desired transparency and individual colouring of the product. Often even costly precious

metals are used in the process. Virtually all red and lilac shades, for example, can be achieved only through the addition of gold. Crystals (for use in chandeliers for example) contain a large amount of lead, hence the term 'lead crystal'. The lead gives the glass its clarity. The special cut often creates a sparkling light effect.

Even today the technique of cutting, like virtually all other glass processes, is carried out by hand. Glass moulding is still an important trade. The craftsman uses a pair of pliers (to a certain extent these are now reinforced by compressed air) to cut individual beads or stones off a length of pre-heated glass. In this process the tool forms the rough shape of the bead which is then tumbled and polished by machine so that in the end the bead is smooth. Allowing for the amount of work involved, even larger glass

Metallic and rainbow-coated glass beads (1)

Cut crystals, some with iridescent coating (2)

Ceramic beads with different glazings (3)

Even the use of the basic colours of white and black in plastic offers a surprising variety of possibilities (4)

Gold and silver-plated plastic beads can be used in many ways (5)

4

5

beads are relatively inexpensive. The hand-shaped items are more costly. Heated glass is wound around a rod; the flow determines the way the colours develop and the shape of the bead. These days in Western Europe individual manufacture of this kind is found almost exclusively in small workshops in Murano.

Attractive effects can be produced on glass beads using a whole variety of metallic and rainbow coatings. In this process different metal oxides are applied to the glass which give the bead a shimmering surface.

A word of caution though: these coatings will often not withstand corrosive agents such as are found in soap, perfumes and in our own body sweat.

Very similar processing methods also exist for plastic, which has gained in importance in the manufacture of costume jewellery. Thanks to the use of more and more sophisticated injection moulding and processing techniques, this raw material has long since overcome the stigma of being a cheap alternative. When buying something made of plastic though, you should take a careful look at the quality of the workmanship, because it only needs one small item to have conspicuous burrs to spoil the overall appearance of the piece of jewellery. High quality products are injected with a variety of additives such as glitter and metallic powder; the burrs are then usually all removed afterwards by tumbling and polishing.

The most expensive plastic elements are frequently made from sheet material, such as perspex, either cut or milled. The price is justified when you consider that this often involves a great deal of hand-work.

Metallic coloured plastic beads are very important for higher quality pieces of jewellery. The ones we have used in this book are always electro-plated. Plating baths may contain high proportions of precious metals. Cheap quality beads are sometimes just spray-painted and are easily scratched.

Plated plastics will never be able to entirely replace beads made of metal. Metals of very different alloys can be used to make sturdy and often very lightweight jewellery elements (round beads, bugles and curved tubes of various lengths, discs and cones). In particular metal beads can be coated with silver, gold or copper in a simple process which gives them a durable finish.

In addition to these more 'traditional' materials there are of course many others which you can use for your costume jewellery. There are no limits to what your imagination can come up with.

Accessories and findings

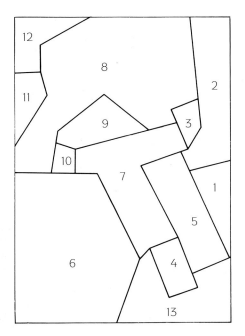

If you enjoy making jewellery, you will need to buy certain basic accessories. Wire is a must: for most pieces of jewellery, 0.6-mm thick silver or copper wire will suffice. It is also advisable to have two further gauges, 0.4 mm and 0.8 mm, in your stocks.

. . . for necklaces

Your basic requirement will always be a cord or a length of thread. Various thicknesses are available. Nylon thread, 0.35 mm thick, can be purchased in bead and craft shops.

Some necklaces, particularly those using light beads, require bead stringing silk. Choose an appropriate thickness for the type of bead. Stringing silk does not lie quite as stiffly as nylon thread.

In some shops you can obtain fine steel wire in a nylon cover. This is highly suitable for heavier necklaces or for threading metal parts. Tiger tail, as it is called, is available in most bead shops.

Calottes are used to conceal the finishing knots of the thread. We prefer using the type which is threaded after the last bead. The knot is then tied in the bowl of the calotte. Since the calotte is threaded in front of the knot, it cannot really slip. This risk is only present in the type which is folded round the knot or stuck down to finish off the end. These types of fastening are, however, quite useful when small repairs are required.

Now a knot tied in nylon thread will not hold well because it comes loose very easily, which is why we slip a bead crimp on to the thread and close it with a pair of pliers. Silk

and the tiger tail we mentioned before can be sealed in exactly the same way.

Leather thonging is suitable for many styles of jewellery and it is available in a whole range of designs and colours. Rubber and PVC thongs are also highly attractive for necklaces.

Necklaces made from any of the thonging mentioned above are obviously thicker than nylon thread and will need a different type of fastening. Crimps that can be clamped over the cord are particularly easy. There are for example small cylindrical leather crimps for cords up to a maximum thickness of 2 mm or alternatively special rubber crimps of different sizes which have small barbs on the inside.

Similar pieces are also available for sticking down the ends. Small caps can be stuck directly on to thick cord to fasten it off and large ones are useful for 'incorporating' multiple rows on one necklace (strung on thread, leather or rubber).

Necklace fastenings come in an almost overwhelming variety. Bolt rings and jump rings are probably the most common type of fastening and these are available in many different diameters. Make sure when you are buying that the open ring closes again automatically and that there are no metal burrs obstructing the mechanics of the fastening.

We have illustrated only the most common barrel fasteners. We would advise against fasteners where the screw is badly finished or too short.

Snaps are very useful particularly for bracelets, because you can close them with just one hand. Snaps with a safety clip to prevent the bracelet from slipping off, should the lock come open, are also available.

Accessories and findings shown:
1/2 Calottes 3 Bead crimps
4/5 Cylindrical leather and rubber crimps 6 Caps 7 Bolt rings and jump rings 8 Barrel fasteners 9 Barrel snaps 10 Hook clasp (swivel) 11 Jump rings 12 Linking bars 13 Clips and scrolls.

In addition there are box catches, hook clasps (swivels) and countless decorative necklace fastenings.

If you are making a big necklace, you should pick a large fastening and not just for optical reasons. A small one is hard to get hold of amongst heavy beads or cords.

You will normally need jump rings to fix a fastening and we would advise against picking soft and thin ones.

In some shops you will be able to find link bars for feeding several threads on multiple necklaces, plus the matching end spacers.

If you want to make a multiple necklace using leather or rubber, you may need scrolls or clips. If you use double-row clips, you will be able to hold more than two cords if you are following an offset pattern. This is quite useful for making belts.

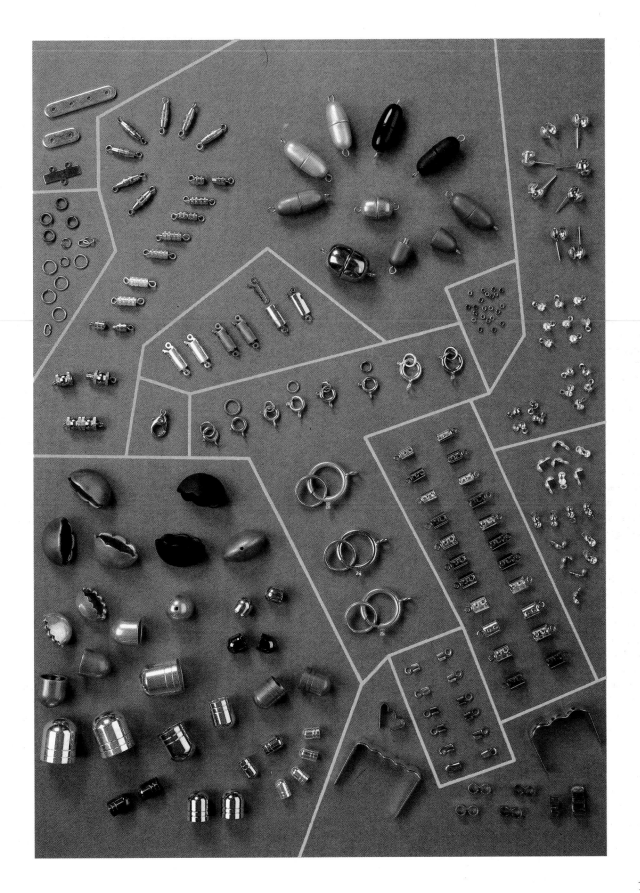

. . . for earrings

Virtually all types of ear pendants will require some form of ear wires. Whether you use just simple curved wire hooks, more ornate open hooks with a small ball on them or decorative silver fastenings, they should be in keeping with the style of the jewellery.

Heavier items should be fastened with earclips. A good clip should have a firm spring but should neither pinch nor slip off your ear (badly formed fastener).

If your ears have not been pierced, there are various devices which can be used. Apart from a wide variety of clips, there are ear-screws, which are particularly suitable because their fine thread allows them to be individually adjusted. In this way you can wear any earring you like.

An alternative to the simple hook is the earstud with ring attachment which will conveniently take longer ear pendants.

Flat-fronted ear fittings are very popular for smaller pieces of jewellery, enabling you to stick on stones, or flat-backed shapes. With very large decorative stones this type of fastening does not always fit properly on your ear and in this case we would recommend an earclip which incorporates a ring which the pendants can be hooked in to.

To make an ear pendant, you will need several small pieces of wire. Head pins are very useful. These are wire pins of varying lengths with a small head at one end (similar to a dressmaker's pin). The head of the pin is used to secure the bottom bead on the pendant. Often the beads have such large holes that they just slip over the pin, so you either have to use a small glass bead in addition or a bead cap. Occasionally different sizes of decorative bead caps are also used as part of a piece of jewellery.

If you want to make the pendant longer than the head pin, though, or if you want it to dangle freely, you will have to bend the top end of the head pin into a small ring and then continue, using an eye pin. This simply hooks into the ring. A totally different shape of earring is the Creole, either in the shape of a ring or an eardrop. These are also available as ready-made wire rings, on to which you thread the beads the way you want them. Other useful accessories are ready-made jump ring shapes, bails for laterally drilled ear-drops and bell caps for stones without holes.

. . . and for brooches

Brooch pins come in a variety of designs. As well as the simple bar illustrated here, there are pins with larger flat fronts which provide a larger adhesive area. Always opt for those pins with a safety catch though!

Perhaps you could try using tie pin findings (also called stick pins) for smaller items. You can glue on to the flat front; the pin stem with its guard often looks quite decorative.

You can do striking embroidery on brooches and brooch backs. However, this technique has been dealt with in many other books and so we will not go into it here.

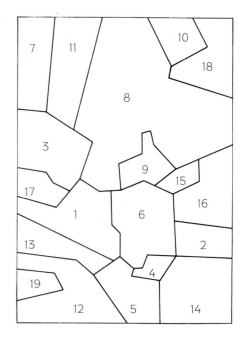

Accessories and findings shown:
1 Ear wires 2 Clips 3 Ear screw 4 Ear studs 5 Flat-front ear fittings 6 Head and eye pins 7 Bead caps 8 Creoles 9 Jump rings and triangles 10/11 Bails and bell caps 12 Brooch pin backs 13 Tie pin findings 14 Brooch back with perforated front 15 Small ear clips 16 Clips with flat front and ring 17 Metal barrel with ring 18 Bridges or end spacers 19 Press studs

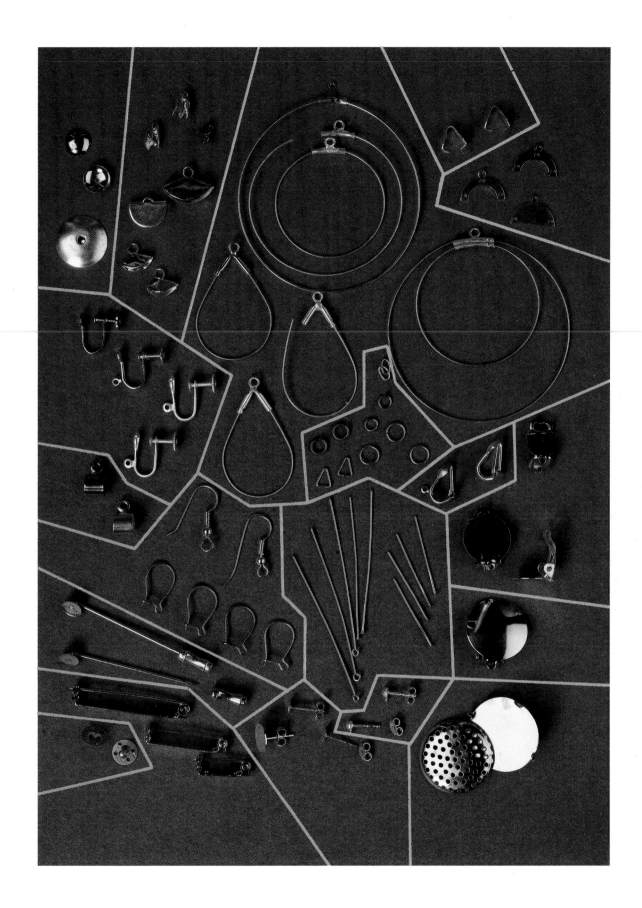

Where can I buy the materials?

This is a question you will perhaps have repeatedly asked yourself as you flicked through the book and read about the different materials.

For us of course this was easy because with our wholesale facilities and our bead shop, our sources were unlimited. Specialist bead shops will be able to offer you the greatest selection and these can normally be found in most big towns, although they are sometimes tucked away in small side streets.

Larger art shops often stock more exotic accessories, not just in pre-packed assortments but also as individual items. More and more shops are also now tending to keep a wide variety of loose beads and art departments of larger shops fall in this category.

Often when you are looking for more unusual items you find things in soft furnishing shops which are not at all intended for jewellery. They also stock the cheapest nylon thread and certain accessories. Shops with a large stock of buttons are also a treasure-house of striking items to use as a base. We give you various tips for incorporating buttons into your jewellery.

When it comes to tools, though, we recommend you purchase these in a proper hardware store, where you can also obtain brass washers and nuts, plus chrome-plated or plastic tubes. Many of these items can be adapted for use.

When you are buying look out for the different quality features which we refer to for many of the items.

Our models are only intended as ideas for your own creations. Usually what happens with a piece of jewellery is that you find a few rather striking stones or beads and then you have to look for suitable items to go with them. Sometimes

you can find what you want in your own little jewellery box – an old chain, which you no longer wear anyway, can be taken apart and the individual links used. Often at the flea market or on a street stall you can find cheap chains which may be very tasteless in their design but which contain very attractive individual elements. With a few trimmings you can soon create an entirely new piece of jewellery. You should always have a small stock of fasteners, wire and thread at home for such occasions.

Tools

In our book we have deliberately chosen only those techniques which you can copy using a minimum of tools. Your basic equipment should contain: round-nosed pliers, preferably with a cutting edge, a pair of snipe-nosed pliers and a pair of household scissors.

The thinner and smoother the finish on the tips of the round-nosed pliers, the more suitable for fine work. If your pliers have rough edges, they will scratch any wire you are using and that does not look attractive. If these pliers also have a cutting edge, this is very helpful for shortening wire, because you then do not have to keep changing tools (and you don't have to have a pair of cutting pliers). When you are purchasing pliers, hold them up against the light: the jaws of the cutting edge should close tightly and run parallel *(top left)*.

You should carry out the same kind of check when you buy a pair of snipe-nosed pliers, because here again the points of the pliers should close as tightly as possible along the whole length of the tool. Choose pliers with flat smooth inner jaws *(pliers with yellow handles)*. You will often find electronic pliers on sale but these are expensive and too lightweight for our purposes.

Sometimes end cutting nippers are quite useful for shortening wire but you really won't need them often *(bottom right)*.

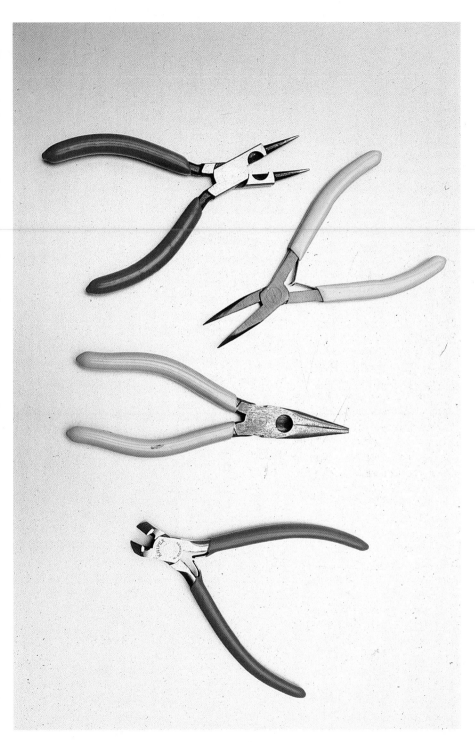

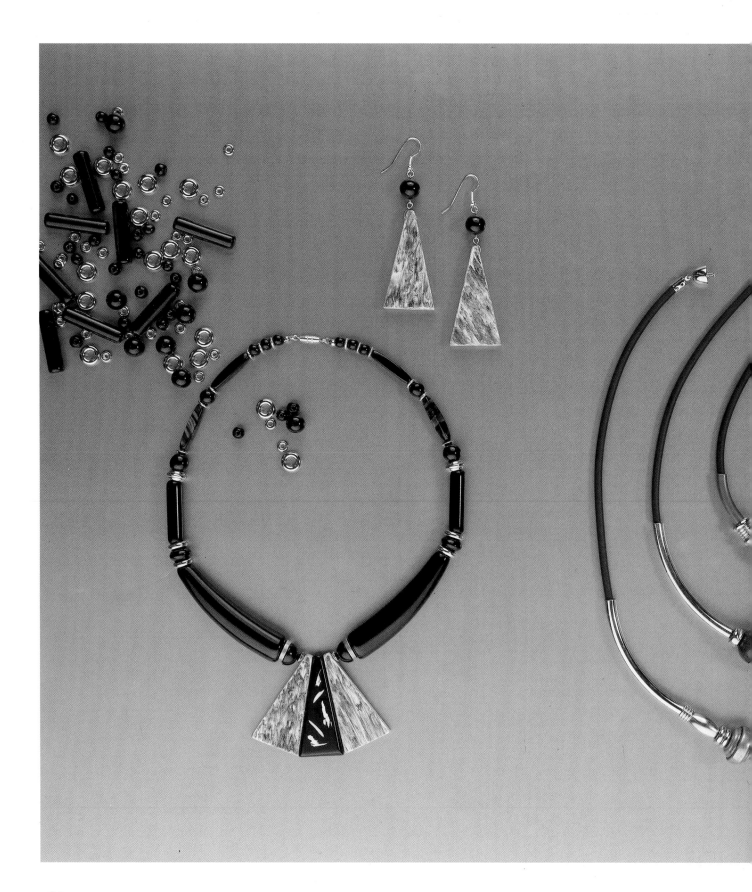

Basic techniques

On the left hand side of the photograph is a definite eye-catching combination: the necklace pendant is made up of three hand-milled triangles.
All the items on the right hand side feature different materials which were deliberately used sparingly. The bangle is made of hat elastic. The three necklaces have been threaded asymmetrically on to rubber and a combination of fine metal tubes and plated plastic beads has been used.

Single rows of beads

The most common form of necklace is the single row of beads on a thread. You can take virtually any bead available for necklaces which use thread. If you select metal or glass beads, where the holes have sharp edges, make sure you pick a strong thread. With silk you may find it necessary to make a knot between each bead.

As there are no restrictions to speak of from the point of view of material, you can let your imagination run free when you are threading single strings of beads. The examples shown here are just to give you ideas.

You should, however, always bear the following details in mind: it is wisest to start with the most eye-catching part of the necklace (this is usually also the centre-piece) and then look for suitable beads to go with it. Thread the beads from the centre to both ends.

A necklace will lie better if it is not threaded too stiffly. It will be stiff if the fastening is mounted too firmly or if beads with very large sides (for example, large disc segments) are threaded next to each other, so when you are making a necklace, you should keep holding it up as it will lie round your neck to see the way it is going to look when it is finished. Towards the ends of the necklace you can use plainer items, providing they are in character with the style.

There are various ways of attaching the clasp, depending on the type of necklace. The illustrations on page 19 indicate the main techniques.

Basically you have to assume that a knot at the end of a nylon thread will not hold. There are a few somewhat doubtful tricks for fixing a knot (singeing it briefly with a lighter, using a drop of glue on the

loop), but the most reliable method is to insert a crimp at the end of the thread. To do this you can either make a simple loop and fasten it off with a bead crimp or you can fit a calotte, threading it after the last bead, then fixing the crimp inside it. The description given assumes the use of a pierced calotte, which is what we would recommend.

You can use other types of calotte which you fold over or stick on to the end of the bead crimp which you have already squeezed over the thread. However, if the job is not

Try out variations of our models! Here you have the same set twice – a single string necklace and ear-drops, using almost identical beads in different shades.

done properly, you may well find the calotte will rapidly work loose. We prefer to use this technique for repairs (for example, on strings of beads where the string has snapped close to the fastening). You can use the technique shown step-by-step on page 19 for all types of thin threads.

18

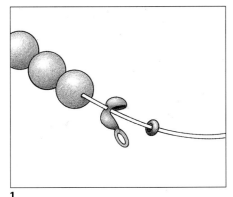

1

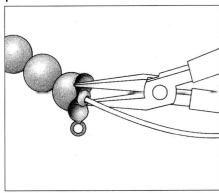

2

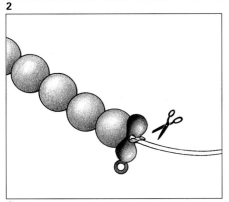

3

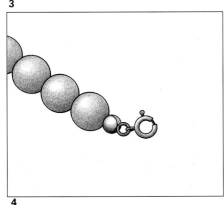

4

Once you have threaded the necklace beads in the order you want them, thread a calotte after the last bead and then a crimp (**1**).

Use a pair of all-purpose pliers (as pointed as possible) to fix the crimp inside the clasp. Make sure on the second end of the thread that the calotte is as close as possible to the last bead but that it does not fit too tightly (**2**).

Make sure that the little crimp can no longer slip around and only then should you cut off the remaining thread and carefully close the calotte over it (**3**).

Now that you have fitted calottes to both ends, you can attach their loops to those of the fastener. To do this carefully open the side of the loops on the necklace fastener or on both the calottes using all-purpose pliers. Link the loops together and close with pliers (**4**).

Please note:
Sometimes you can buy clasps and fastenings where the ends are soldered; for these you will also need sturdy wire jump rings.

There is an easy trick for making knots close to the last bead on the string. You make a loose loop and then you put a needle or a stiff piece of wire through this, so that the knot is wrapped round the needle. Hold the end of the thread with one hand and with your other hand pull the needle, and with it the knot, towards the last bead.

Tip:
If you are using beads with larger diameters (for leather) as well as other beads with very small holes all on the same necklace, you may well find it irritating that those beads with large diameters always hang out of line. An easy trick: fill in the large holes. Thread small glass beads on to the necklace and slip the beads with the large diameter over them. You can use this same trick with wire, for example, when you are making earrings.

You can also slide hat elastic through larger holes. It is particularly suitable with bangles, as here you simply make a knot between two beads. Even if the bangle does not have a fastening, you can just slide it over your wrist.

It is equally easy to thread beads with large holes on to leather thongs or rubber strands. You don't need to cover the entire band, because the end crimps can happily be left showing. In some cases one can opt for fastening leather with a plain straightforward knot, although the metal crimps available are easy to fit and give a neat finish.

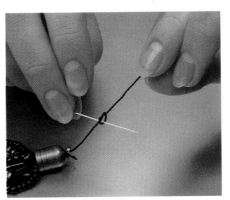

Necklaces of exceptionally fine beads.

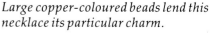

Large copper-coloured beads lend this necklace its particular charm.

Page 21: *Chains made from just a few different materials often look extremely aristocratic through their very simplicity. The piece on the top left is made up of two sizes of the same black and white travertine bead and coconut discs of different sizes in three colours.*

The necklace on the right is made simply of cubes and black rods. Plain wooden beads can also be used to create interesting jewellery. The mauve and violet set, for example, is made entirely out of wooden components.

The bracelet at the bottom of the page is made once again using hat elastic, and can also be worn as a necklace.

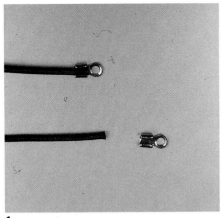

1

2

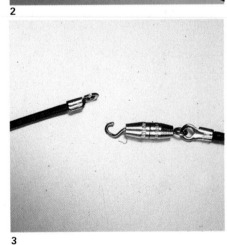

3

The end crimps commonly used for leather and rubber thongs are basically identical; the instructions apply to both.

When you have threaded your necklace, push a leather crimp on to each end of it (1).

Using the snipe-nosed pliers press one side of the clip to close it, then the other side. Never press both sides down at the same time because in order to close tightly, the sides should overlap as far as possible (2).

You can usually open the rings on the fastening. These jump rings, which open sideways, should then be hooked into the leather crimps and sealed again. If this fails, you will have to use small jump rings to fit the fastening (3).

The spiral-shaped crimps just need to be pushed over the end of the band (4).

They can be fastened with a drop of glue or the last curl of the spiral can be pressed together with the pliers (5).

Try the crimps to see if they actually hold. The best way to do this is to hold the ring with a pair of pliers and pull carefully at the thonging. Clearly they will not withstand a firm tug but they should be able to cope with twice the weight of the necklace (6).

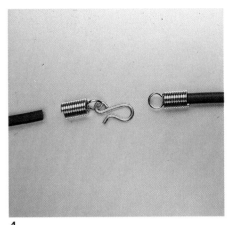

4

5

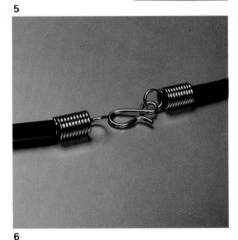

6

Page 23: Hand-made, matt glazed ceramic beads threaded on a leather thong with a few coconut discs make an unpretentious necklace.

Rubber thongs are made in many different colours. Here white is shown, threaded with white and jade-coloured rings, together with several metal pieces. You can combine the most varied materials without any stylistic incongruity. The grey necklace is made up of ceramic, wooden, plastic and gold-plated beads.

You can also acquire spiral-shaped end crimps for leather and rubber thonging. These are more in keeping with certain styles.

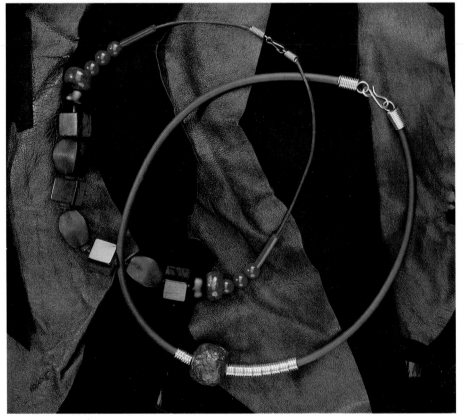

Strong leather thongs can be obtained from the shoe mender's. Brown leather for example is used as a drive belt for the sewing machine.

The long dangling wooden beads are each hung on a knotted leather loop which is in turn threaded on to the necklace, with the knot supporting the bead.

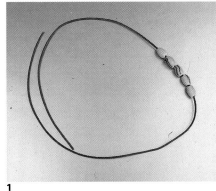

1

If you tie a knot in the leather, you avoid having to fit a fastening. At the same time you can vary the length of the necklace by adjusting the knot.

Once you have threaded all the beads, lay the ends of the leather parallel to one another (**1**).

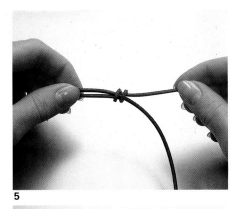

5

Hold both ends of the leather between thumb and index finger of your right hand so that one end sticks out at the top of your right hand. Make sure this end is long enough (**2**).

2

Using your left hand make a loop round the thumb of your right hand. The end of the leather sticking out at the top of your right hand is then fed under both leather strips (**3**).

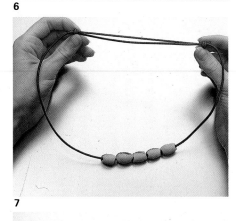

6

Using the same method make a second loop round your thumb. Take your left thumb and push the double loop slowly and carefully off your right hand. Hold this loop firmly between your left thumb and index finger so that with your right hand you can pull the end of the leather through the loop towards you (**4**).

3

Hold the two ends of the leather with your left hand. Using the thumb and index finger of your right hand pull both ends of the leather until the knot forms and is pulled tight (**5**).

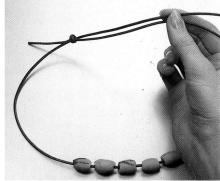

7

Turn the entire necklace round. Now hold the leather strip between your thumb and index finger so that the end of the leather sticks out over your right hand. Repeat the knot as described before (**6**).

4

The ends of the leather strip can be cut off just after the knot. If you want to make the necklace shorter, pull the knots apart. If you take both hands and pull at the individual strips just after the knot, you can

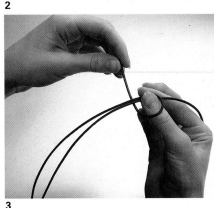

8

extend the length of the necklace and it will be easier to slip it over your head (7).

A variation would be to just make a knot at one side by folding back the end of the leather and then making the knot as described before (8).

Again the ends will now have to be shortened and you can adjust the knot by holding the leather thong in one hand and tightening the knot with the other.

It is not necessary for every necklace to have a fastening. If you are using a leather thong, making a knot in it will enable you to adjust it to the right length. The large beads are made of wood and are hand-painted.

Simple earrings

If you follow the step-by-step instructions given on page 29, you can make virtually any kind of earrings. Pages 12/13 give you details of the necessary accessories and findings.

An earring which is meant to hang straight down must have a fastening under the last bead. You will have to either thread the beads on to a head pin, where the pin head holds the bottom bead in place or form a ring or loop yourself to stop it from falling off.

Earrings dangle more effectively when they are made up of as many links as possible, so thread your beads on to several short pieces of wire and make a ring or loop at both ends. By hooking the various pieces into one another you create your ear pendant.

You will find the techniques described in the instructions. Only at the end do you hook the ear wire into the top ring. It is entirely up to you whether you choose clips, wires, hooks or ear-screws.

*You can wear all these earrings even if your ears are not pierced. **From left to right** the special devices used are an ear-screw, a wide surface clip, a small clip.*

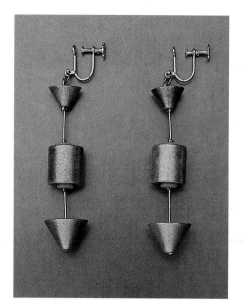

Incorporate various links into your earrings – that way they dangle much better.

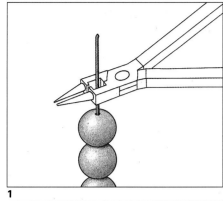

1

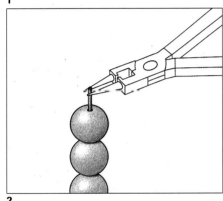

2

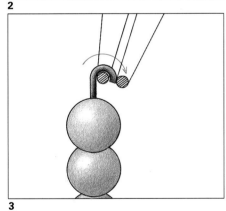

3

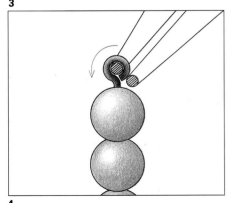

4

Once you have threaded all the beads on to the wire, cut this off leaving about 6 mm above the last bead (**1**).

Hold the end of the wire with the ends of the pliers and bend it to form a small ring or loop. Keep the wire firmly curled round the ends as you do so, because then the round edge of the pliers makes the shape of the ring (**2/3**).

Adjust the ring so it is in the centre by bending it back slightly (**3/4**).

The final wire ring or loop should be closed approximately in the middle above the last bead. If another element has still to be hooked into it, the ring should only now be opened up again slightly to accommodate this (**4**).

Instead of using special bails for laterally drilled holes in ear-drops, you yourself can make a dainty mounting as follows: insert a piece of wire through the hole and bend both ends of the wire straight upwards. Shorten the wire at both ends (preferably with one single cut) to around 12-15 mm (**5**).

Use round-nosed pliers to bend each of the ends outwards to form small rings (**6**).

Hold both rings with the ends of the pliers and press them together so they lie flat on top of each other. Here we have threaded the wire with crystal glass ear-drops; to make them longer we added an eye pin which was hooked into the previously-made mounting (**7**).

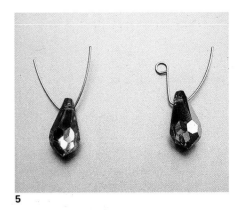

5

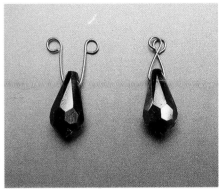

6

7

Creoles

Instead of making ear-pendants you can also make a hoop, which is referred to as a creole. You can make creoles if you have a small roll of wire which has no kinks in it.

Cut a ring off the roll of wire and bend one end outwards at right angles. Thread the beads carefully (so that the wire does not get unnecessarily bent) from the other end (**1**).

You can then use the round-nosed pliers to form the first small ring or loop at the end where you began threading the beads. When it is completely closed, this can be hooked over the other end. To do this just slide the ring over the top of the wire end until it lodges in the bend (**2**).

Now shorten the bent section of wire to the correct length for a ring or loop, hold this end with your pliers and form the ring. You will have to work very precisely because the creole will look odd if there is surplus wire between the bend and the ring over and above the length needed by the ring formed by the other end of the wire (**3**).

Now all you need to do is to bring the upper ring into line a little and possibly adjust the creole circle and fit an ear wire (**4**).

When putting together the beads for the creole you must bear in mind that longish beads are unsuitable for the ring shape. If necessary bend the wire slightly so it is shaped like a drop.

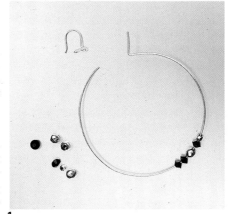

1

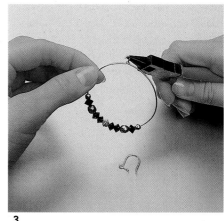

3

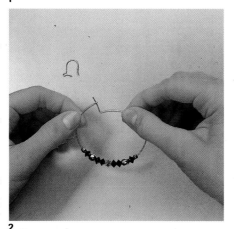

2

4

30

Ready-made creoles will always be open on one side. Push the wire apart carefully on the side to enable you to thread the beads in the order you want them (**1**).

Once you have arranged them as they should be, push the wire back into its fastening, making sure it is inserted deeply enough (**2**).

Now close the fastening on the open side by pressing it firmly together using a pair of pliers. You can tell by looking at the fixed section of the creole how the finished fastening should look. Finally hook in the ear wire (**3**).

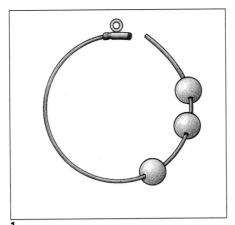

1

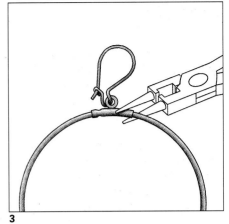

3

2

Creoles threaded with little rondelles and sequins. At both ends of the sequins bead crimps have been pressed on to the wire so that the centre piece with the sequins does not slip about.

The creoles in the photograph below show you how attractive sequins look when used in jewellery. They also look very effective when threaded to make a necklace; threading them is just a matter of patience. Before you start, though, you should at least determine the way you want the colour shades to run so that you can pre-sort the sequins accordingly. If you make mistakes when threading them, it can be very annoying.

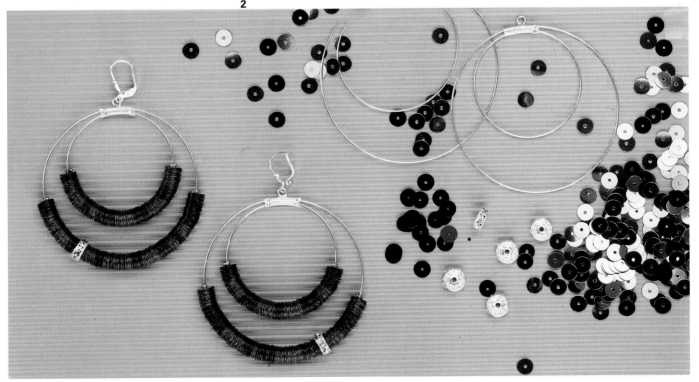

Instead of using wire, a thicker band made of leather or rubber is also suitable for making creole-shaped earrings. Special findings are available for the top fastening.

If you are using wire to make creoles, avoid picking over-large beads. That way you enhance the filigree effect of the slender rings.

Page 33: Creoles made of black rubber look particularly dressy when combined with metallic-coloured beads. The ear-drops at the top of the page are just fastened together with large leather crimps.

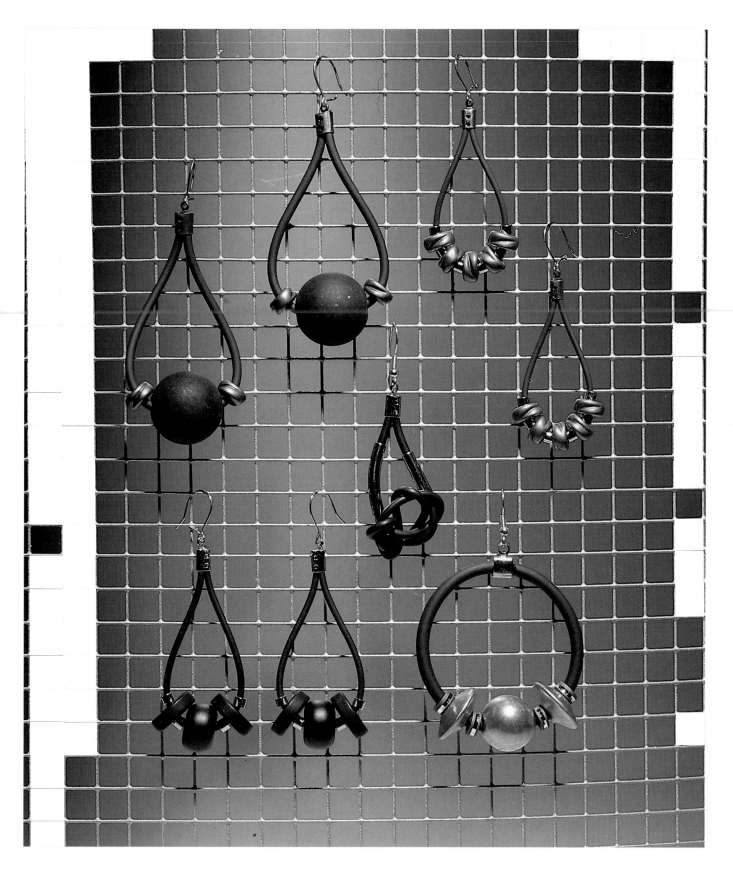

Ear-clips and ear studs

Mother-of-pearl also looks very elegant as an ear-clip or ear stud. All the examples in the picture are made using old buttons. Sometimes in shops of long-standing you can find real Art Nouveau or Fifties collectors' items which you can buy very cheaply. Buttons with shanks are also suitable for many ear-clips. If the shanks are stuck on, you can usually remove them just with the aid of a pair of jewellery pliers, without damaging the button. The discs with the matt shimmering surface are made from mink shells – hand finished souvenirs from the South Seas (*top*).

It would be virtually impossible to envisage the world of costume jewellery without paste and shimmering rhinestone gems. The glass rocks and nuggets shown here can normally be obtained in shops specialising in Tiffany glass art. If they are used for earrings, they should only be glued on to clips, because of their weight (*centre*).

Little paste stones look very fetching as discreet ear studs. The metal-coating on the reverse of the stones is very sensitive. Enquire in your local glass shop about a special adhesive (*below*).

Look for suitable stones or shells washed up on the beach on your next holiday which you can use in jewellery-making.

34

Basically you can use almost any flat item for making ear studs and ear-clips. You just have to keep an eye out for the right item.

Paste gems can be glued on to dramatically enhance a simple piece of jewellery. It only takes patience and careful application.

On the left we have used copper beads and concealed the hole using a small triangular plate with inset imitation stones.

On the top right are two glass buttons in the style of the Fifties and below them are modern buttons made of striped plastic.

Items pierced at the edge can be easily made into clip fastenings.

Suitable adhesives and how to use them

When you are making jewellery you will no doubt have to use adhesives. At this point we should like to give you a little technical information with regard to their use.

Essentially it is true that with an all-purpose adhesive you can stick anything but it does not always stick well. It is wiser to opt for an adhesive which is specially designed for the material you want to stick.

Of all the 'all-purpose adhesives' the hard-bonding type is the one we find most suitable for jewellery. Especially when used on leather or wood, and also on metal, we have been quite successful with several products.

In addition to special adhesives, there are two very different kinds which we find extremely suitable for use in jewellery-making: superglue and two-component adhesive.

Superglue

This is an adhesive on a cyanogen acrylate base, requiring clean and speedy work. It takes two to three seconds to bond, which means that alterations are only possible within limits. On the other hand it does not produce any strands or filaments and once things have been glued together, they stay in position and do not slip about. It takes about two to three hours though for the adhesive to harden properly.

There are many different superglues: one 'universal' type and countless special adhesives. They vary principally in their viscosity, by which we mean the degree of their liquidity. The higher the viscosity value, the less liquid the adhesive. This is frequently vital in use because on the one hand a highly liquid adhesive runs out rapidly on the sides yet on the other hand it forms a much thinner adhesive layer.

A highly liquid adhesive is unsuitable for wood, leather and cork because it penetrates the pores too deeply instead of forming a film on the surface.

Usually glues with a higher viscosity value will require a longer reaction period. This means you have longer to make amendments. Thicker adhesives are also useful for levelling out small cracks or uneven surfaces. This type of adhesive should however be applied very carefully because under pressure it tends to swell out between the parts which have been glued.

For fine work on visible surfaces, such as applying small paste stones, we recommend using a highly fluid glass and porcelain adhesive. If you want to glue large items together and fasten brooch pins and clips to the back of jewellery, the best adhesive to use is a more viscous glue.

The most important point to remember as preparation for using all types of adhesive is that the area to be glued must be free of grease. In most cases acetone is very suitable for the job. When you are working with superglues, you should always have some acetone close at hand, because it dissolves the glue again. This is most helpful if your fingers get stuck together! Acetone does however attack many types of plastic and paint finishes so severely that the surface immediately becomes matt. In such cases we use nail polish remover with as few oil additives as possible. There is also a special cleansing agent (acetone-based) for rapid adhesives which does not attack plastics quite as quickly. It is useful for rectifying glueing mistakes or for removing excess glue. Dab it off with a paper tissue. Superglues also dissolve at temperatures over 80°C, so with heat resistant materials sometimes a cigarette lighter helps.

In order to avoid accidental contact with the adhesive, you should always lay one of the pieces you want to glue flat on the table and apply the glue to this. Then you can attach the other piece. Remember to always read the safety precautions on the packet. Always keep adhesives out of the reach of children!

Two-component adhesives

These adhesives are produced on an epoxy resin basis. They contain a resin and the appropriate hardener. The two components only start to work when they are mixed together in the proportions indicated.

Two-component adhesives have a much higher viscosity than superglues, in other words they are less liquid. They offer an adhesive film which can level out very uneven surfaces and larger cracks. They are on the other hand very unsuitable for delicate work.

Two-component adhesives are somewhat awkward to use, because you always have to mix a certain quantity in a given ratio. Since you then need a maximum of 20 minutes for it to work, it is wise to consider beforehand the shapes you wish to make and the way you want to arrange the items to be glued. Your work should always be well prepared. Usually the hardening process of epoxy resins starts after 45 minutes but some adhesives require twelve hours before they are fully hardened. That means that you cannot move the finished item for quite a while. So-called epoxy putty is easier to use. This is made up of two components, a white and a black stick which both look like normal plasticine. You take approximately the same amount from each stick and knead the pieces together with your hands until an even grey mass is formed. You can then apply it with your fingers and press it into wide cracks. When applying, make sure you do not spread it too thinly. Remove excess with a knife while the mixture is still soft. Since epoxy putty is very viscous you can continue working with the freshly glued piece if you are careful with it. It needs about four hours to dry, then it is as hard as rock and you can drill holes in it, file and polish it.

Brooches and decorative pins

If you are unable to find the right piece for your ideal brooch, have a look through a shop stocking buttons. If buttons have a shank, you can remove this and on standard buttons you can conceal the holes by sticking something over them.

Small paste gems and pearls are very useful for covering over buttonholes. For precision work you can use a pipette which is screwed on to the bottle of adhesive. If the metal pipette gets clogged up, just hold it in a flame (**1**).

Lay the piece you are working with flat on the work surface and apply the glue in small doses around the edge of the hole. Now carefully place the paste gem on the glue and press firmly (**2**). Make sure you place the stone correctly first time!

Brooch pins should be placed on the back of the piece only when both surfaces have been thoroughly degreased (**3**).

If you have large pieces of jewellery the brooch pin must not be glued in the middle. Place it towards the top otherwise the brooch will fall forwards (**4**).

Buttons can be used for a multitude of purposes without anyone realising their origins. Here are a few examples for clips and brooches.

1

3

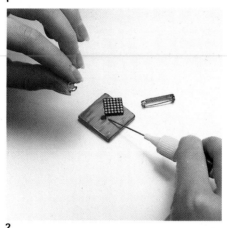

2

4

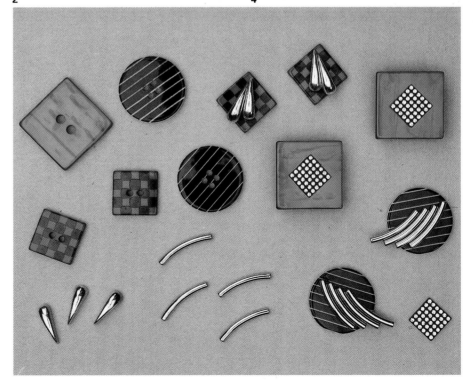

A button with a pierced plastic end-spacer fixed vertically to it. A loop made of rubber has been glued through the holes in this piece.

Tubular beads glued over a button, concealing the hole in the middle.

If you cannot obtain large beads like these for brooches, buy perspex remnants and use a saw to make your own designs. That way at least you can be sure your jewellery is exclusive.

38

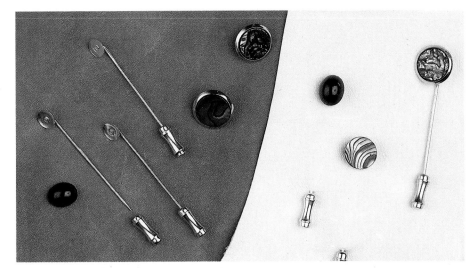

You don't always have to make brooches. These tie pins look very elegant on collars and ties. The protruding guard can be an additional ornament. Here small glass gems, mother-of-pearl and other beads have been glued on to the findings.

If you collect unusual buttons you can always quickly make a special tie pin if you need a little present to take along to someone.

More advanced techniques

The thick multiple-row necklace is made of rubber strands with small metal rings threaded on them. The earrings were made to match. The set with the wider silver tubes looks very exclusive but it is in fact quite quick and easy to make (instructions on page 47).

Multiple-row necklaces

It often requires a lot of patience but as you can see on the following pages, the effort involved in making necklaces of multiple rows is always very worthwhile. If you are using small beads you should use bead silk which has a flexible wire needle attached to it for easy threading. Usually there is more yarn on the card than you need for a necklace of normal length. Unwind the whole thread for stringing the beads and you can keep the needle for threading your next necklace.

Here is the completed necklace, whose composition is illustrated step-by-step on page 43. It is made entirely of small glass beads. An enlargement of the fastening is also shown.

The finished piece can be worn as shown or slightly twisted like the necklaces on the following pages. Open the necklace and twist the rows before you put it round your neck.

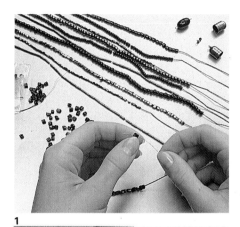

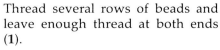

Thread several rows of beads and leave enough thread at both ends (**1**).

All threads are fastened together at the end with a knot. This task is made easier with the help of a needle. In this way the position of the knot can be determined. Hold the ends of the threads with one hand and use your other hand and the needle to pull the knot right up to the beads (**2**).

Leave one thread out and cut the remainder off just above the knot (**3**).

The knot can be further secured with a drop of glue (**4**).

Now pull the remaining thread through a cap, then thread a calotte after it (**5/6**).

Make a knot just inside the calotte. You may find two knots are necessary so that it does not slide over the thread (**7**).

Now that you have fastened off both ends of the necklace as described with caps and calottes, attach a necklace clasp to the loops of the calottes (**8**).

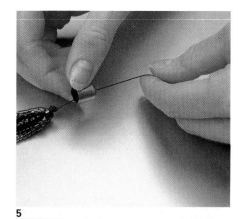

5

6

7

2

3

4

8

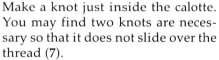

Two almost classical examples of multiple-row necklaces which look particularly attractive when twisted slightly: the top necklace is a blend of simple mauve coloured beads together with iridescent glass beads.

This necklace is made up of different types of plastic olivary beads plated in metallic colours. For this reason the necklace is not too heavy.

Cut crystal refracts the light in many facets. The little glass and pearl beads do not detract from this effect.

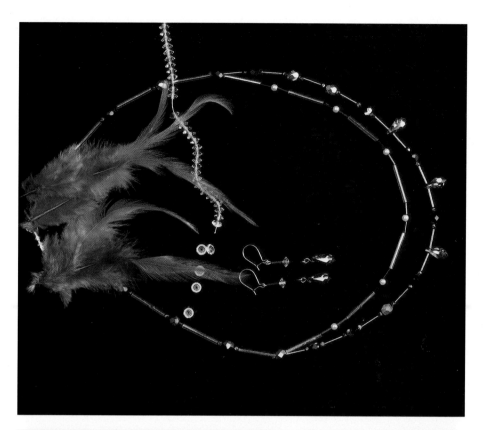

Metal spacers keep these two strings of beads apart. The white slivers are made by hand from plastic. They are particularly effective against the subdued black beads.

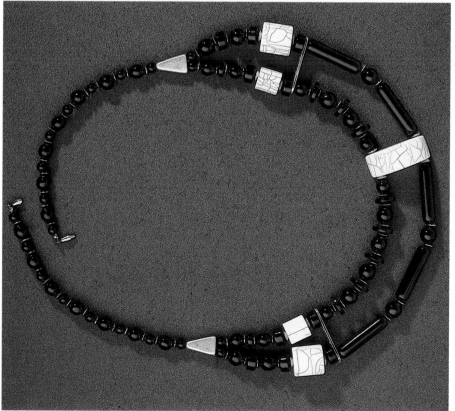

The front sections are attached to the back section by special spacers (inset photograph). Each of the individual rows is attached to the spacer. A fastening was not necessary because the necklace is long enough to go over the head.

46

This striking necklace of leather and small metal tubes has been made according to a well-known technique for glass beads with slight modifications.

Take two leather strands and thread them alternately through the metal tubes. Make sure that the strands cross over at the same points (not first from the left, then from the right) otherwise the necklace will look lop-sided (*photos below*). By putting small metal rings between the tubes the necklace falls in a rounded shape.

Knot the leather thongs after the last tube at either end. Slip a wider metal tube over each knot, adjacent to the other tubes. On each side snip off one strand closely, so that knot and spare end are concealed inside. From here there is only one strand of leather running to the fastening. Above these metal tubes are two round beads to keep the leather in position in the middle of the tubes.

The remaining bits of leather have been used to make a pair of matching earrings. Here again two strands are used at the start. Thread both strands through a wide tube, then bend each strand outwards and up through a narrow tube either side. You now have four strands. Slip a scroll clamp over these strands (two in each loop of the scroll). Squeeze with pliers and cut off one strand on each side, close to where they emerge from the scroll clamp.

A little bit above this on each earring is a plastic olivary bead which has been threaded on and fixed with adhesive. Higher up the leather strands join in a leather crimp attached to the earring.

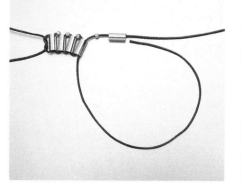

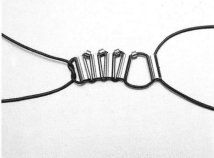

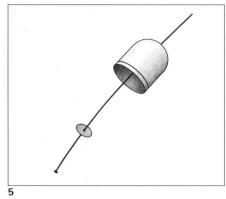

You will need a piece of wire at least 12-15 cm long. Bend the first 5-7 cm of this at right angles. This piece should then be placed in the centre of the strands so that it sticks out over the ends of them and the bend is hidden between them at a depth of about 15 mm (**1**).

From the bend the wire should now be wrapped firmly round the strands working towards the end of the necklace. You should pay more attention to correctly positioning the individual strands around the central wire than to their ends being of equal lengths (**2**).

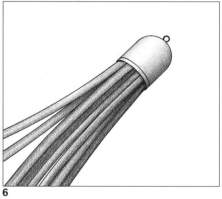

Once you have finished winding the spiral, chop the ends of the strands off evenly just after the spiral with a sharp knife. Put a few drops of glue over the cut ends. The piece of wire protruding is threaded from the middle through the small hole in the cap (**3**).

Push the cap firmly over the strands. Leave enough wire to form a loop and then cut off the protruding wire. Bend the wire to form the loop and attach the necklace fastening (**4**).

Variations in the fastening technique: You can also try glueing the strands directly into the cap itself. With the right number of strands, good adhesive and a grease-free cap (particularly plastic ones) this will also hold.

Since you need a loop on the cap for mounting the necklace fastening, first push a head pin through the hole from the inside. If the head of the pin does not hold, place a small bead or a tiny disc under it. Shorten the protruding piece of wire and make it into a loop with pliers (**5**).

Spread a little glue (possibly using a matchstick) on the inside of the cap and push the strands as far inside as possible (**6**).

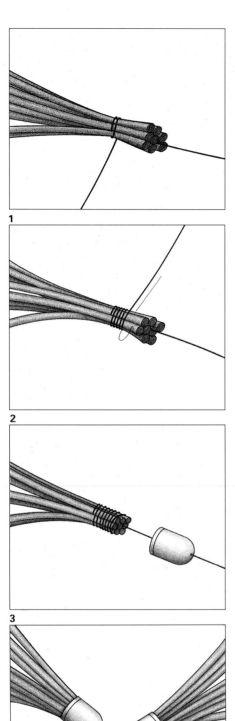

Page 49: Several leather strands with narrow metal tubes threaded on them look different with every new colour combination and go well with almost every style.

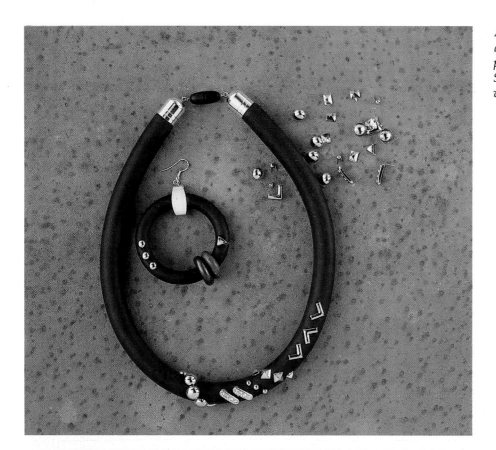

A choker made of rubber with studs attached. The metal pins have been pressed into the soft rubber. Stylistically the creole earring goes well with it.

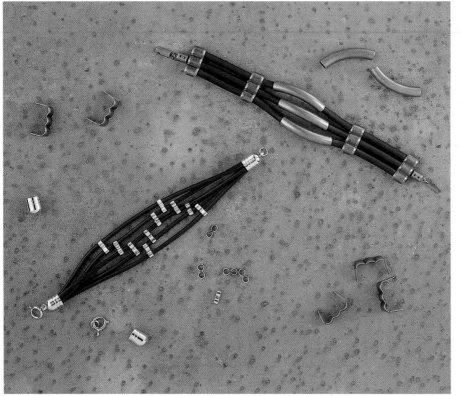

You can also use scrolls to form a bridge from one row to several others. You can attach them by simply pressing them firmly on to the bands. Bracelets are all made according to the same principle.

Page 51: *A strikingly large necklace with a wooden toy dice and macramé bead on rubber strands of varying thicknesses, in combination with silver beads.*

Rayon braids and cords can also be integrated into jewellery. Here they are combined with various metal chains and wound into a knot which is held on the sides by several rings.

Page 53: Simple but striking – this necklace is composed of two thick loops. To make it lots of leather strands were fastened together to make two skeins. These cross over in the middle. We have used black-painted metal chains without a fastening for the back part since the necklace can be easily slipped over the head.

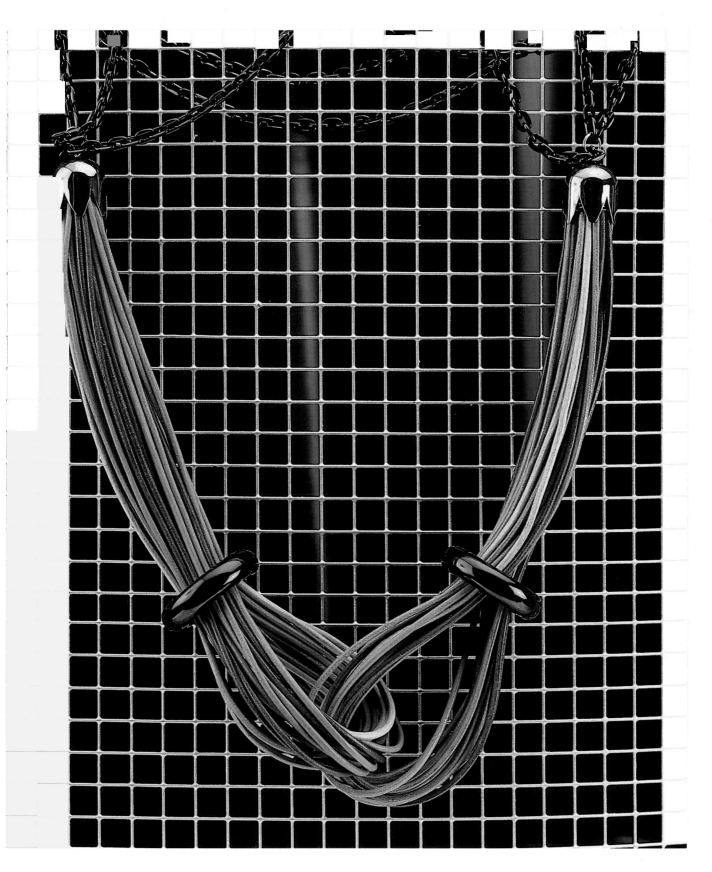

Necklaces made of several rows of beads and large metal items look more dainty if the beads are spread out well on the individual strands. You can do this by fixing each element in position by tying a knot, or you can glue them in place.

First you must ensure that all the beads are spread out the way you want them to be on the final necklace. Place the jewellery on a flat surface and put the pieces in the correct positions. Memorise the pattern because they might slip a little.

Now push each of the beads or metal pieces slightly to one side and apply a little glue all round the spot where they were before.

Push the bead back on to the glued area and press the thonging sideways against the inner wall of the hole. The necklace should then be left for as long as possible without being moved. If the diameter of the strips is in correct proportion to the holes, these fixtures should last well.

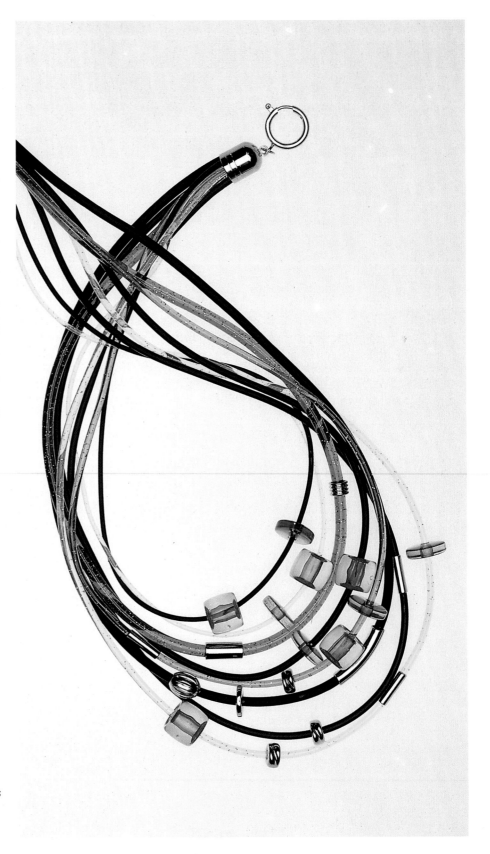

Bright colourful PVC mica-filled bands used in combination with transparent discs and a few black bands where the silver metal pieces have been glued on.

This bright necklace and earrings set with the matt-finished wooden olivary beads was also achieved with the use of glue.

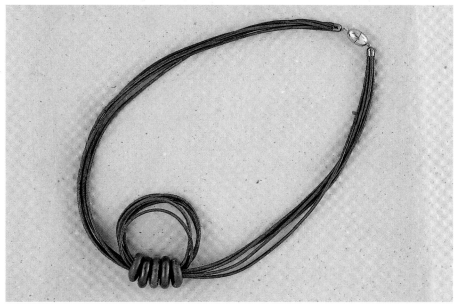

Rings of all sizes are good for holding a loop in place. The loop with ceramic rings should be worn slightly to one side.

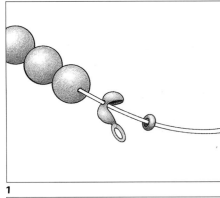

1

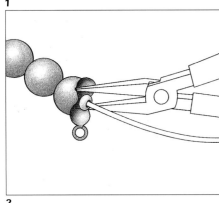

2

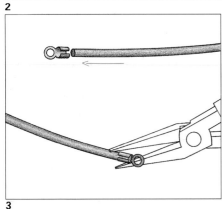

3

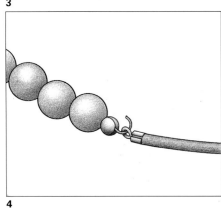

4

If you want to thread beads on to leather or rubber and the holes in the beads are not big enough, you can use nylon thread in the centre of the necklace and connect this to the leather or rubber.

The beaded strand, secured by calottes at either end, may be either attached to two equal lengths of leather which are fastened with a necklace clasp, or to one length of leather long enough to slip over the head.

After the last bead you must first thread a calotte and then a crimp (**1**).

Now close the crimp inside the calotte using snipe-nosed pliers. Cut off the thread sticking out beyond the crimp. Close the calotte (**2**).

Push the leather crimp on to the end of the leather strip and close the sides with your snipe-nosed pliers (**3**).

Gently open the ring of the calotte sideways, hook in the end of the leather strip and close again. Repeat this procedure for the other end of the thread (**4**).

This can be done without calottes if the thread is strong enough.

Thread a crimp after the last bead, then pull the thread through the ring at the end of the leather, feed through the loop and back into the crimp. Pull the thread through the last bead(s) as well and let it stick out on the side between two beads (**5/6**).

Close the crimp at the end of the first thread as soon as the loop is tight enough. NOTE: the loop must still be able to move freely in the leather crimp otherwise the thread will be liable to break (**6**).

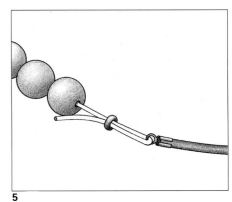

5

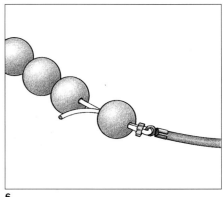

6

You will have to pull the other end of the thread until the necklace is firm enough. Now close the crimp with your pliers and make sure that both ends hold.

Finally you can cut off the thread at either end close to the beads so that the spare ends disappear between them. That way they will not scratch your neck.

Crystal-clear plastic beads with mottled colouring in the middle look particularly attractive against a light background. The ends of the thread were fastened off with crimps to form loops.

Plastic beads can be used to achieve the most striking effects: here a black and white zebra pattern has been used. The coloured discs are all made of dyed coconut shell and calottes are used for the fastening.

Necklaces with a centre-piece made of larger beads should have a sturdy back fastening. Here we have used several parallel leather strands. The dark-coloured necklace is made from buffalo horn beads, black coconut discs and a few gold-coloured plastic elements which add elegance.

The other necklace incorporates bleached coconut discs and mottled brown plastic beads. The fastening has been mounted on the side.

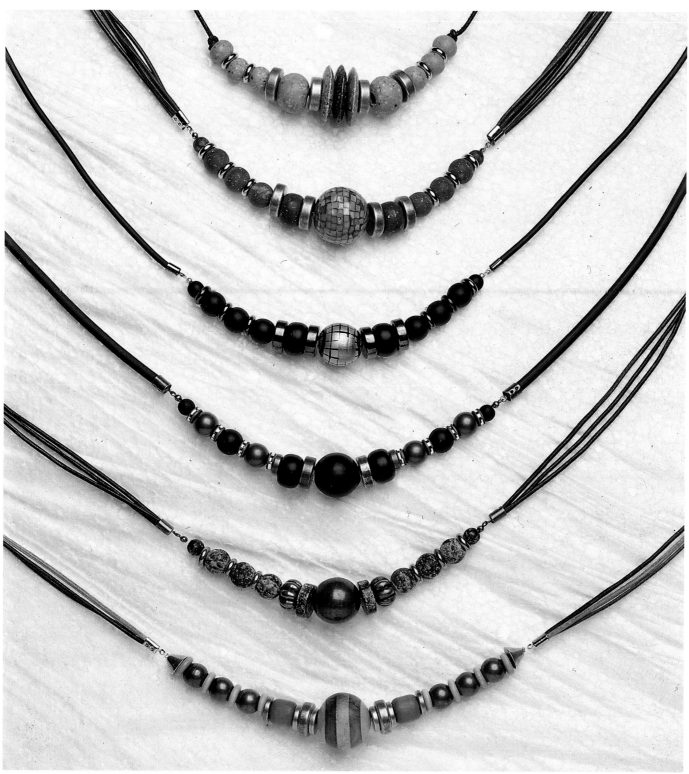

All the necklaces on this page have been made using almost identical beads arranged in the same pattern. On the top necklace we started with ceramic

and silver beads on leather. All the other combinations have a centre section on a nylon thread. (The instructions can be found on page 56).

Each necklace looks different! Once again we should like to point out that all the examples shown are merely intended to prompt your own ideas.

Naturally attractive

Nature has given us a fascinating variety of patterns and shapes: on the left are a few mink shell discs which have been laboriously glued and polished by hand to make the round balls used in the turquoise necklace. In the centre are a few pieces cut from shells. Next to these on the right is abalone, or paua shell, from New Zealand, shimmering in blue and grey.
A necklace made from pointed ends of horn left in its natural state, is shown on the hill.

Beads made from natural materials

Materials and work techniques which go back thousands of years have retained their value to the present day. It is impossible to imagine modern jewellery without elements made from natural materials. The oldest material apart from teeth is bone. For obvious reasons animal horn is also frequently used for making jewellery. Beads made from buffalo horn with their attractive matt black sheen and fine mottling are often integrated into pieces of jewellery; they usually come from Asia (India and the Philippines). A popular combination is with brass or silver beads which are easy to make.

The photograph at the top of the page shows various beads made from natural materials. The matt sheen of the buffalo horn beads stands out well against the smooth surface of the ebony. Often tiny squares made from shells are glued by hand on to plain wooden shapes in a very laborious process. The coloured beads are: discs of mink shells (blue), pieces of bone (red) and dyed corals (yellow).

But the most important natural material is wood, whether it is hand-carved or industrially manufactured as a bead. For costume jewellery, simple untreated wooden beads are ideal for low-cost combinations. On the preceding pages we have often used hand-painted wooden beads. This is the ideal raw material for every type of painted finish. Contemporary designs lend themselves to the production of small quantities of costume jewellery. Complex elements made from several exotic types of wood are real eye-catchers. These can be glued together combining various different shades or, alternatively, turned or carved into imaginative shapes.

Tropical woods are fascinating because of their many different colours. None of the ones shown in the centre picture has been dyed!

The brown wood with the black grain, reminiscent of animal skins, comes from palm-trees (the darker wood from coconut palms). The bead with the added brass strips (at the edge of the photo) comes from India and most of the others have been made by craftsmen on the Philippines.

These techniques are used in the Philippines in particular for a whole range of decorations using almost all the natural materials available, such as mother-of-pearl, shells, corals, fruit-stones and of course coconut shells.

Discs made from coconut shells have been used quite frequently in the pieces of jewellery shown here, the reason being that they are cheap to buy, they are available in every colour imaginable and their somewhat irregular shapes add a special touch to the piece of jewellery.

With the right combinations you can be independent of available imported jewellery and use the materials mentioned; your style will give a different accent to the individual item. Don't hesitate to incorporate plastic and other 'extraneous' elements into your work or to dye natural materials. Our photo on page 62 (bottom) shows how bone discs, corals, shells and clay beads have been arranged in colourful harmony.

If you aim for quality and a harmonious blend, these materials can form an exquisite arrangement.

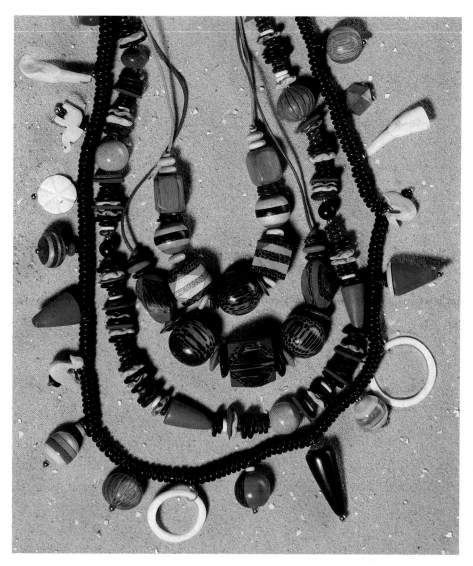

Here you see how natural materials can be combined in various different styles. Most necklaces are composed chiefly of wooden beads and discs of coconut shell. One necklace features a complete collection of different items mounted on head pins: colourful shells, beads made of horn, bone, dyed coral and wood.

A single string made from irregularly-shaped pieces of dyed bone is very eye-catching.

The necklace is asymmetrical but harmonious. The section inserted on the one side and made up of dyed shell plates is balanced out by colourful coconut shell discs on the other side.

Page 65: Black ebony discs of greatly varying shapes have been incorporated into the lower necklace. They are interspersed with coral discs dyed dark blue. The flat dangling pieces of wood have been fastened on with head pins. The whole design gets its sparkle from two cone-shaped beads made of buffalo horn and mother-of-pearl shells. The hexagonal tubes made from pieces of shell are a striking feature in the middle necklace and have been glued on in combination with small discs of bone dyed red. On the third necklace a hand-carved ebony ball has been used in combination with a few ceramic beads, two old African glass beads, two small yellow coral discs and some ebony discs.

Feathered jewellery

Light, downy, lively, delicate, in exotic colours and patterns – feathers are ideal for bringing lots of variety into jewellery. Whether you wish to make dainty earrings or an impressive brooch, nature has provided a fascinating range to suit every purpose.

On this page you can see a tiny selection of coloured feathers: the small fluffy ones are marabou feathers, the narrow red ones are from golden pheasant chicks, the beige ones with dark spots from guinea fowl; less exotic feathers are from ducks, geese and roosters.

They are easy to use on smaller pieces of jewellery. You can use chain parts of necklaces as accessories. Viscous adhesive is recommended for glueing, requiring a longer setting time. You should always remember that feathers are very delicate.

A beautiful brooch made with tightly packed ostrich feathers and long delicate silver filaments. The warm colours come from plant dyes. The quill ends are held by two triangular leather pieces, decorated with a shimmering mother-of-pearl button.

1

2

3

4

To make earrings you could for example wrap wire round the feathers, the way we showed you on page 48 for leather strands. For larger numbers of feathers use an end cap and glue them into this (**1**).

The rings or loops are made in the way explained on page 29. You can also hook beads into the fixings using a head pin or the ear wire can be mounted directly (**2**).

Smaller numbers of feathers can be fastened with a piece of rubber or a large calotte. A drop of glue can be added to ensure that the fitting stays firmly in place (**3**).

When pressing the leather crimps together, make sure that the feathers do not end up at an odd angle. Protruding quill ends can be cut off afterwards with a knife (**4**).

Secure selected feathers with a combination of a flat-backed decorative shape and small piece of leather to make a fine feather brooch. The brooch pin will adhere firmly to the leather (**5**).

Using a leather remnant (or a piece of strong foil) cut out the chosen shape and fix the feathers to it with adhesive (**6**).

Now glue this piece behind the decorative front plate so that the feathers rest between the piece of leather and the plate. Protruding quills and leather can be trimmed off with a pair of scissors. Finally fasten the pin on to the back with adhesive (**7**). One example of what you can do is shown in the bottom photo on page 66.

5

6

7

Feathers can be used to make lots of different pieces of jewellery. It is the trimmings which determine the style of the feathered piece, as you can see from these two photographs.

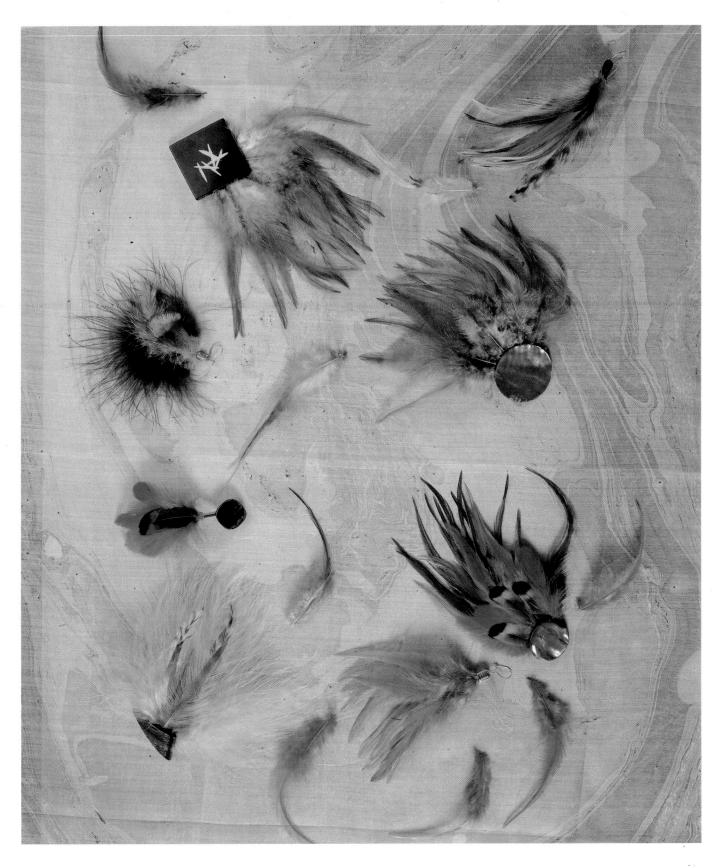

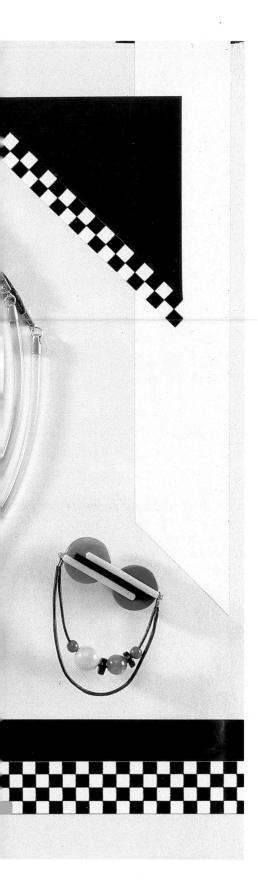

Variations on a theme

The pieces of jewellery on this page are actually just made of simple beads and wire; what is required most is time. To start with you should have a very clear idea of what shape you want to make and then you have to find the right components for the style. The black wire has been covered by a thin PVC tube (which you can obtain from an electrical shop). You can also use cable insulation. The wire should not be too thin otherwise it will bend easily. It has to fit firmly in the tube because it also has to hold the beads. The rest is just a question of patience and practice.

The necklace combines many different elements and exploits the potential of various accessories and findings. Pre-planning and patience, the virtues mentioned above, are also required to make up a necklace like this. The brooch on the outside right is a variation on the clips on page 38. Head pins were inserted through the holes of the diagonally glued tubular beads and these were bent at the ends to form loops. Dangling leather strips were then attached with beads threaded on them.

One more hole

What you need to know about using a drill

As time progresses you will no doubt find more and more unusual ideas for the design of your own personal jewellery. This can often be triggered off by a single piece which you have seen somewhere. You start thinking of the different options for adapting it and mentally arrange other items to go with it. You might then find you require linking elements which the materials do not offer. The answer is often a small, light drill.

If you just need to enlarge a small hole in a wooden bead or turn a button into a piece which can dangle, a light DIY-drill with electronic speed regulator or a battery-powered screwdriver with chuck will no doubt do the job. However, a hammer drill is not suitable, because its weight might well crush a delicate part. It is also far too difficult to work accurately with it and there is an increased risk of injury.

A small, light 12 volt drill with a separate transformer is the ideal instrument for jewellery-making purposes. The speed of the transformer can be regulated to accommodate the type of material being drilled, which makes the machine very versatile.

There are now a whole range of accessories for this little machine, including special drilling stands, vices, milling and sanding heads, polishing devices and mini-jigsaws.

Regardless of the type of drill you decide to buy, a stand is to be recommended under all circumstances. Once the drill is held firmly in position on the stand, it cannot slip while you are drilling because it is guided vertically.

If you have the piece you are working on held firmly by a vice (or at least in a clamp), nothing should really go wrong.

A few tips on better drilling:

You will have to select a certain speed for almost every type of material. Almost all drills run too fast on full speed, so the drill gets hot, you burn out the drill head and it becomes blunt.

You may also damage your material if you are too hasty in your drilling. Wood gets brown burn marks, certain plastics melt and clog up both the drill and the hole. If you are working with hard metals, take a break every now and again so the drill can cool down or apply a little oil at regular intervals (sewing machine oil is perfectly adequate). Hold the drill without applying much pressure; that way the hole will be clean.

On delicate materials it is wise to cover the clamps of a vice with textile adhesive strip. Each item you are working on must be held very firmly so that it cannot slip or slide out. If necessary back it with a piece of wood. If you do not have a vice, you should at least work on a firm surface and make sure the item cannot slip about.

You should avoid using glass unless you have a special diamond drill and sufficient experience.

Once you have acquired a small 12 volt drill, you should use its capabilities to the full. With the milling head in particular you can modify designs and transform surfaces in many ways.

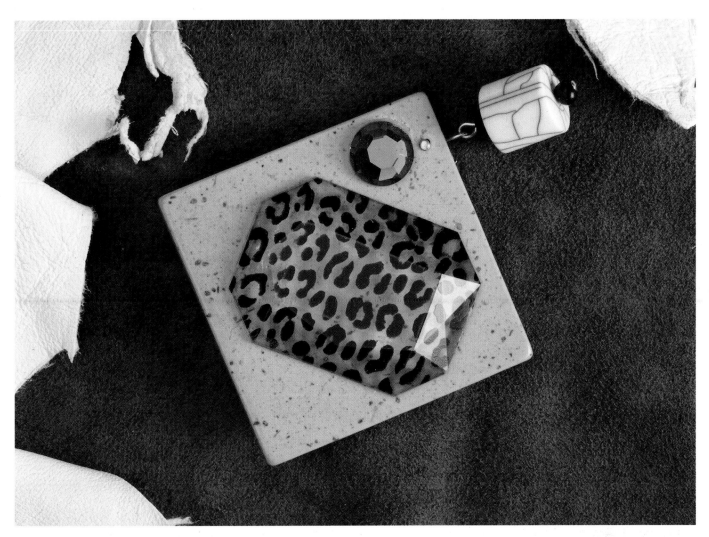

A mixture of materials with a brooch as the end product; to make it even more eye-catching we have drilled a hole in the brooch, hung a head pin in it, from which a bead now dangles.

Two more examples of earrings. On the right is a pair of creoles made of rubber tubing; continental clips are used in the dropper earrings on the left.

A home-made FIMO piece was used here for the base. This modelling clay can be hardened by baking in the oven. Two holes have been drilled in the top edge and a rubber thong has been glued into them. A semi-circular button has been stuck to the back of the FIMO shape.

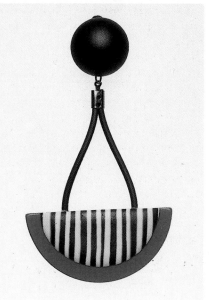

You can obtain foils and small mirrors of all shapes and sizes on haberdashery counters. These can easily be made into decorative brooches and clips with a few feathers, stones and buttons.

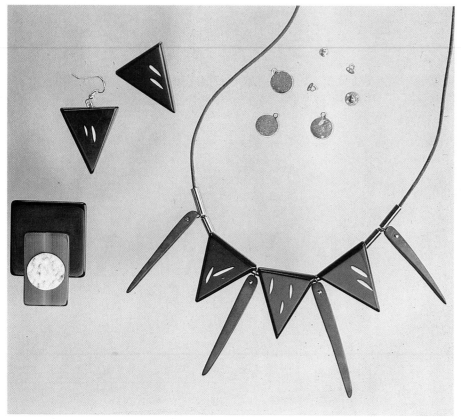

Metal press studs or old button shanks are ideal for fastening flat-backed shapes without holes on to necklaces. Glue one or two button shanks to the back of shapes like these triangles, and pass the necklace thread through the loops behind. The coconut teeth are fastened to the necklace with head pins.

Page 75: *Here again we have glued press studs behind the flat discs.*

Buttons and beads teamed up with attractive earring findings.

Page 77: The choker shown is highly practical: the ball end used as a fastening can be unscrewed. Then the beads can be threaded on to the wire. You don't have to fill the entire ring.

Black glass and fluted gold beads dangle from a decorative triangular spacer which is hung from a golden earclip.

The other pair of earrings uses end caps such as are found on the ends of leather necklaces. Hanging from them are lots of thin metal chains held together on a ring.

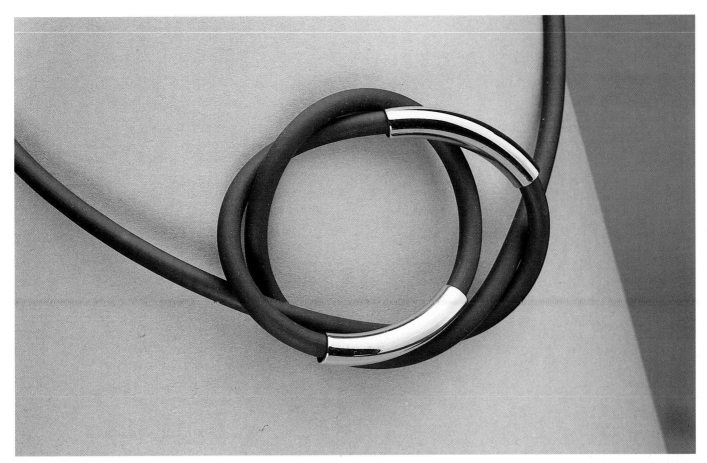

Fine metal tubes and imaginatively looped rubber create a very striking necklace.

Two sets of earclips, simple in design but striking in their effect. Here holes have been drilled in plain flat-backed shapes and the large drops have been attached with jump rings or head pins.

Page 78: Two more necklaces using hand-painted wood.

A selection of striking brooches, using a variety of materials

Acknowledgements
Photographs Dietmar Seip, Cologne
Photograph on page 6 Ulrich-Klever-Archive, St. Georgen
Line drawings Ulrike Hoffman, Bodenheim.
English edition consultant Maureen Murray

U.K. sources of findings, threads, wires, tools and catalogues:

The Bead Shop
43 Neal Street
Covent Garden
London
WC2H 9PJ
01-240 0931

The Bead Shop
21 Sydney Street
Brighton
East Sussex
0273 675077

Ells and Farrier
20 Princes Street
London
W1R 8PH
01-629 9964

Hobby Horse
15/17 Langton Street
London SW10 0JL
01-351 1913

First published 1989 by The Hamlyn Publishing Group Limited, a division of the Octopus Publishing Group, Michelin House, 81 Fulham Road, London SW3 6RB

First impression 1989

Copyright © 1988 Falken-Verlag GmbH, 6272 Niedernhausen/Ts. West Germany

Copyright © 1989 English translation The Hamlyn Publishing Group Limited

ISBN 0 600 56386 3

Typeset by Dorchester Typesetting, Dorchester
Produced by Mandarin Offset
Printed and bound in Hong Kong